My First Animal Library

Ostriches

by Penelope S. Nelson

Bullfrog Books

Ideas for Parents and Teachers

Bullfrog Books let children practice reading informational text at the earliest reading levels. Repetition, familiar words, and photo labels support early readers.

Before Reading

- Discuss the cover photo. What does it tell them?

- Look at the picture glossary together. Read and discuss the words.

Read the Book

- "Walk" through the book and look at the photos. Let the child ask questions. Point out the photo labels.

- Read the book to the child, or have him or her read independently.

After Reading

- Prompt the child to think more. Ask: Did you know about ostriches before reading this book? What more would you like to learn about them after reading it?

Bullfrog Books are published by Jump!
5357 Penn Avenue South
Minneapolis, MN 55419
www.jumplibrary.com

Library of Congress Cataloging-in-Publication Data

Names: Nelson, Penelope, 1994– author.
Title: Ostriches / by Penelope S. Nelson.
Description: Bullfrog books edition.
Minneapolis, MN: Jump!, Inc., [2020]
Series: My first animal library
Audience: Age 5–8. | Audience: K to Grade 3.
Includes bibliographical references and index.
Identifiers: LCCN 2018039326 (print)
LCCN 2018040673 (ebook)
ISBN 9781641285612 (ebook)
ISBN 9781641285605 (hardcover : alk. paper)
Subjects: LCSH: Ostriches—Juvenile literature.
Classification: LCC QL696.S9 (ebook)
LCC QL696.S9 N45 2020 (print)
DDC 598.5/24—dc23
LC record available at https://lccn.loc.gov/2018039326

Editor: Jenna Trnka
Designer: Jenna Casura

Photo Credits: Iom66/iStock, cover; Eric Isselee/Shutterstock, 1; Coffeemill/Shutterstock, 3; Mark Dumbleton/Minden Pictures/SuperStock, 4; gorsh13/iStock, 5; Guy Dekelver/Getty, 6–7, 23bl; blickwinkel/Alamy, 8–9; Andrzej Kubik/Shutterstock, 10–11; NHPA/SuperStock, 12; Luis Tejo/Dreamstime, 13, 23br; ottoduplessis/iStock, 14–15; xpixel/Shutterstock, 16; Vasiliy Vishnevskiy/Alamy, 17; Doug Cheeseman/Getty, 18–19; JanJar/Shutterstock, 19; EcoPic/iStock, 20–21, 23tl; Aaron Amat/Shutterstock, 22; NaturePL/SuperStock, 23tr; GlobalP/iStock, 24.

Printed in the United States of America at Corporate Graphics in North Mankato, Minnesota.

Table of Contents

Speedy Birds

Zoom!

What was that?

An ostrich!
It has strong legs.

They are the fastest
runners of all birds.

They run from predators.

Like what?

Lions. Cheetahs.

cheetah

They hide, too.
They put their long
necks down.
They are harder
to see.

Ostriches are the biggest birds in the world!

They can be nine feet (2.7 meters) tall!

They have wings.
But they cannot fly.
Why?
Their bodies are
too big and heavy.

What are their wings for?
Steering!

They eat plants.

What else?

Bugs. Lizards. Snakes.

They even eat rocks.
Why?

They do not
have teeth.
Rocks break
down food.

17

Moms lay eggs.
They are big!
They will hatch.

ostrich egg

chicken egg

19

The chicks will be fast
like mom.

chick

Parts of an Ostrich

eyes
Ostriches have the largest eyes of any land animal. Each one is almost two inches (5 centimeters) across.

feathers
Ostrich feathers are not waterproof like other bird feathers. They get wet in rainstorms.

wings
Ostriches use their wings to steer while running.

toes
Ostriches only have two toes on each foot. This helps them run faster. All other birds have three or four toes.

legs
Ostriches have large, strong legs that help them run fast.

Picture Glossary

chicks
Young birds.

hatch
To break out of an egg.

predators
Animals that hunt other animals for food.

steering
Guiding or directing.

23

Index

To Learn More

Finding more information is as easy as 1, 2, 3.

❶ Go to www.factsurfer.com

❷ Enter "ostriches" into the search box.

❸ Click the "Surf" button to see a list of websites.